Starting Out

Ken Moser

Published in 2013 by 10Publishing, a division of 10ofthose.com

9D Centurion Court, Farington, Leyland PR25 3UQ, England.

Email: info@10ofthose.com Website: www.10ofthose.com

ISBN 978-1-909611-40-5

Printed in the UK

Starting out:
Contents

leader's notes available through
www.effectiveyouthministry.com

Starting Out:
Introduction

Welcome to Starting Out!

Being a Christian is a tremendous thing. We have a God who forgives our sins and loves us! This is great news.

Over the next six weeks you will be going on a journey that will cover a lot of ground. You will explore a number of great things that the Bible teaches about starting out in the Christian life:

- » You will see that God shows his love for us by sending Jesus to die on the cross.
- » You will examine what it means to live by faith in God.
- » You will find out how you can be sure that you are going to heaven.
- » You will look at what the Bible says about dealing with sin in your life.
- » You will discuss how to stay a Christian for your whole life.

Being a Christian is an exciting road to travel. My hope and prayer is that by the end of this series of studies you will be a strong (or stronger!) follower of Jesus.

Enjoy the next six weeks!

Ken Moser

Starting Out: Becoming Friends With God

For God so loved the world that he gave his one and only Son, that whoever believes in him shall not perish but have eternal life. John 3:16

If someone asked you, "How do you get to know God?" What would you say? (Circle your answer)

Go sit in the forest

Carve a statue of God and bow down to it

Don't really know

Ask your grandmother

Read the Bible

Get on your knees and crawl to the nearest church

Try to do good things to please him

Ask for forgiveness

Something else ______________________________

going deeper

God loves us! **Read John 3:16-18.**
What did God do for us? (v.16-17)

What must our response be? (v.18)

Go to Jesus to get eternal life! **Read John 3:36.**
What happens if we don't care what God did for us?
Have you ever heard this message before? When? How did you respond?

What are the responses some people make to Jesus? (Circle your answer)

Jesus, who's he? *A good guy, but who cares!*
I don't want to hear about Jesus! *I'll think about it later!*
I'm not ready to change my life! *Believe and have life!*
God loves me regardless of whether I believe in Jesus or not!
I'd follow him anywhere! *Other* ____________________

What does John 3 say about these responses?

Jesus tells us that the correct response to what God has done is to "repent" in order to enter God's Kingdom. **Read Mark 1:14-16.**
Do you know what the Kingdom of God is? (Who is the King? Who are the subjects?)

What does it mean to repent? (✔ your answer)

- ◯ To pent again!
- ◯ To cover something with more paint
- ◯ To stop doing something
- ◯ To stop, turn around and go in the opposite direction
- ◯ To say 'sorry'
- ◯ Hmm, don't know

What is the connection between repentance and having a relationship with God?

Why is it so necessary?

If someone asked you, "Why do we need to repent of sin?" do you think you could answer them?

brainwork **Hey, aren't some people "good enough to go to heaven"?** This is a common question as not all people appear to be totally evil. It seems unfair that God doesn't let some people into heaven based on being "good". **Read Romans 3:10-18.**
How do you feel when you read this list?
Is there anyone who hasn't sinned (see v10-12)?
What do v. 13-17 tell us about human nature?
What is lacking in all people according to v. 18?
How do you think God feels about the fact that everybody is a sinner and has "turned their back" on him?
If there is time, read Romans 5:6-8.
What is God's solution to our not being 'good enough' to go to heaven?

getting active

Helping each other
How can this group help each other to understand and respond to God's love?

Is there anything that we must do differently this week in light of our study today?

let's pray

- Thank God for showing us that he loves us by sending Jesus to die for us.
- Pray that each person in this group will know that God loves them.
- Pray that we will never take God's love for granted.
- Pray for friends who don't know God's love.
- *Other things we can pray for*

____

____

stay tuned

Next week we will learn about what it means to have faith in God!

For your eyes only:
The week ahead

For your eyes only:
The Week ahead

1. Have you turned from a life of sin to a relationship with God?

It may be that after this study you now realize that you need to repent of your sins and come into God's Kingdom. If you want to turn and make God the king of your life there are a few simple things you must do.

1. It is very important that you repent of your sins. This means admitting that you have done wrong asking for forgiveness and turning away from a life without God.
2. Here is a simple prayer you can pray: "Dear God, I am sorry for living a life apart from you. I am sorry for all the things I have done that are wrong. Thank you for loving the world so much that you sent your one and only Son. I thank you for his death on the cross for me. I want to now live as a child of yours. Please help me to do this as long as I live. Amen."
3. If you do this, God will forgive you completely. Jesus died on the cross for this very reason!
4. After you have prayed this prayer, you should tell your Bible study leader. He or she will be really glad to hear this!
5. It would also be helpful to read the box below (The Good News is really good!) and read the Bible verses. These verses drive the point home about why the death of Jesus on the cross is so important.
6. If you pray this prayer, make sure you keep going to Bible study to learn more about Jesus and how to live the Christian life. Being a Christian isn't simply praying a prayer of forgiveness and then doing what you'd like. Following Jesus must have a big impact on your life. Reading your Bible with other Christians will help you to understand what it means to follow Jesus each day.

2. Personal Bible Reading

This week, try to spend some time reading the Bible. You can do one of two things: either read the sections from the Bible dealing with the good news of the gospel (you'll find these in the box at the bottom of this study) or begin to read the gospel of Mark. This is a great book about Jesus and what he's done for us. See if you can read chapters 1-4 this week.

My weekly Bible reading plan!

In the gospel of Mark I read (place a ✔ when you have read it!)

Chapter 1 ☐ Chapter 2 ☐ Chapter 3 ☐ Chapter 4 ☐

Hot tips for those who are just starting out and have never read the Bible!
The Bible is a great book. In fact, it is really a collection of books (66 in all). There are two main sections to the Bible: the Old Testament and the New Testament. The Old Testament was written before Jesus, the New Testament was written after him. It will take you a lifetime to get to know the Bible really well, so be patient. Try and take one section of it (for example, the book of Mark) and spend some time getting to know it well. Read it a few times. Make sure you ask God to help you to understand it each time you read. Keep a notepad handy and write down any questions you have. You can ask these questions to your Bible study leader or your minister when you see him/her. Have fun!

3. Memory Verse

A great way to get to know what the Bible teaches is to memorize Bible verses. Can you learn the memory verse at the top of the study (John 3:16)? Give it a try this week.

4. Prayer

Spend some time each day thanking God for all the good things He has done for you. Make sure to thank Him for the "good news". That is, the fact that Jesus has died on the cross to pay the price for your sins. Pray for any friends or family that don't know Jesus yet. One simple way is to make two lists: things to thank God for and things to ask God to help you with. Make a list of things under the headings below and spend some time this week in prayer.

Things that I can thank God for: ______________________

____

____

Things that I need to ask God to help me with: ______________________

____

____

The Good News is really good!
The clear teaching of the New Testament is that we were like "sheep going the wrong direction". However, Jesus died on the cross to pay the penalty for this and to lead us back to God. This is good news! (This good news is often called the "gospel".) There are a number of Bible verses that tell us about the gospel. Here are some for you to read and think about. As you do, you will soon realize why the good news is so good!

Mark 10:45	John 3:16 & 3:36	Romans 5:6-8 & 6:23
Colossians 1:21-23; 2:13-15	2 Timothy 1:15	Titus 3:3-8

Starting Out: Faith

Now faith is being sure of what we hope for and certain of what we do not see. Hebrews 11

let's get started

let's get started

1 What do you put your faith in? (Choose as many as you like from the list below and share your answers)

- ◯ My family
- ◯ My own strength & talent
- ◯ Myself
- ◯ Other? ____________
- ◯ My school
- ◯ My friends
- ◯ God

2 Do any of these sentences describe you?

- ☐ I only believe in what I can see or feel
- ☐ I'll never believe in God unless I see him for myself
- ☐ I've just started to believe in God
- ☐ I've believed in God my whole life
- ☐ Sometimes I believe in God but sometimes I don't

God loves faith! **Read Hebrews 11:1-6.**
Verse 1 describes faith as two things. What are they?

1. ____

2. ____

What does faith enable us to do? (v. 3)
Read verse 6 again. What does this verse tell us about faith? Why is it so important?

Has there ever been a time when you doubted the existence of God? Why? Why not?

The rest of Hebrews 11 contains a list of people who had strong faith in God. Take a look at four of them.

a) Abel v.4 (Genesis 4:1-10)

b) Enoch v.5 (Genesis 5:21-24)

c) Noah v.7 (Genesis 6:9-22; 7:6-10)

d) Abraham v. 8-12 and 17-19 (Romans 4:1-3)

More stories about faith: **Read Hebrews 11:32-38.**
How do you feel when you hear about these people's faith?

How can we be more like them?

____

____

____

brainwork

Faith=Action!

Have you ever met someone who says that they have "faith in Jesus" but then doesn't act like it? The Bible tells us that faith in Jesus must be seen in action. **Read James 2:14-24.**

What does this tell us about faith? What is the relationship between what we believe and what we do? Read v. 19 again. In light of this verse, what should you say to someone who says that they have faith but then doesn't act like it?

(You can read Matthew 7:21-27 for more on this topic.)

getting active

getting active

Helping each other

How can we help each other to trust in God more and more?

How can we show our friends and family that we have faith in God?

Is there anything that we must do differently in light of our study today?

let's pray

- That we will be people who live by faith.
- That our faith will be seen in what we do.
- *Other things we can pray for* ____________________

____

____

stay tuned Next week we will look at the question, "Can I be certain that I am going to heaven?"

For your eyes only:
The week ahead

For your eyes only:
The Week ahead

1. Personal Bible Reading

How was your Bible reading last week? Did you set aside some time to read God's word? If you started Mark, you should be up to chapters 5-8. Make sure you ask God to help you understand His word.

My weekly Bible reading plan!

In the gospel of Mark I read (place a ✔ when you have read it!)

Chapter 5 ☐ Chapter 6 ☐ Chapter 7 ☐ Chapter 8 ☐

FYI

What is the Old & New Testament? The Bible is split into two big sections. The Old Testament is the first part and deals with the nation of Israel. (This is the Israel of thousands of years ago, not the modern day one). It starts with the creation of the world and is full of great stories about our spiritual ancestors like Abraham, Noah, Moses and King David. It is full of well-known and loved stories. While it is big and can be hard to understand in parts, it is well worth the effort.

The New Testament is about Jesus and the group of people who followed him. It begins with four gospels, each telling the story of Jesus. Then comes the Book of Acts, which is about the early church. This is followed by a number of letters that various people wrote to encourage and help Christians to follow Jesus. Remember, it will take a lifetime to really get to know the Bible well, so start today!

2. Memory Verse

Can you learn the memory verse at the top of the study (Hebrews 11:1)? Give it a try this week.

Now faith is being sure of what we hope for and certain of what we do not see. Hebrews 11:1

3. Prayer

Spend some time each day thanking God for all the good things He has done for you. Make sure to pray that you will always have strong faith in Him. Pray for any friends or family that don't have faith in Jesus.

Things that I can thank God for: ____________________

____

____

____

____

Things that I need to ask God to help me with: ____________________

____

____

____

____

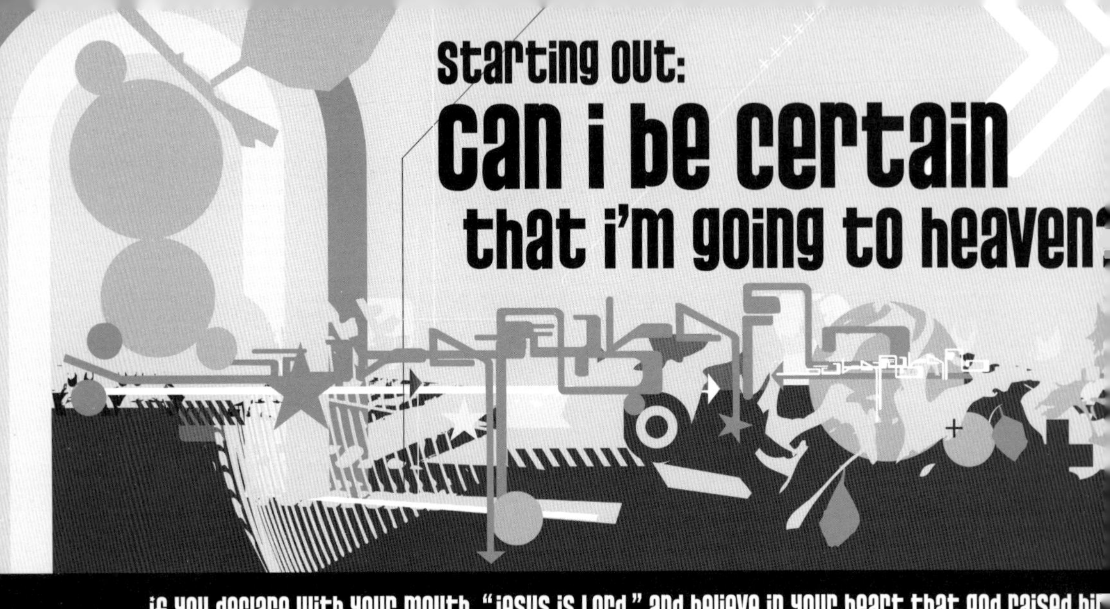

Starting Out: Can I be certain that I'm going to heaven?

If you declare with your mouth, "Jesus is Lord," and believe in your heart that God raised him from the dead, you will be saved. Romans 10:

let's get started

let's get started

1 How certain are you that you are going to heaven? (Place a mark somewhere on the line)

1 -- 100

No way — I think so, kind of! — Yep, absolutely

2 One day your friends say to you, "Can you be absolutely certain you are going to heaven?" How would you answer them?

____

____

____

____

If you trust in Jesus, nothing that can separate you from God's love! **Read Romans 8:31-39.**

What does this passage from the Bible tell us about God's attitude towards us?

What does the promise of v.38 & 39 mean for us?

In light of this passage, how would you answer someone who says, "You just can't be sure that God loves you and you are going to heaven"?

The Bible says we can know that we are saved!

Read Romans 10:9-13.

What two things must we do to show we are saved? (v.9)

What is the difference between the two?

What happens when we do these two things? (v.10)

What is the promise of the Scripture according to v. 11?

In light of this Bible passage, what would you tell a Christian friend who begins to doubt that they are going to heaven?

You're in safe hands! **Read John 10:27-30.**

What are the two things Jesus' "sheep" do? (v.27)

What is the promise that Jesus gives to the sheep? (v.28)

What does this tell us about Jesus? The Father? Us?

In light of this passage of Scripture, how can you keep trusting in God's promises?

brainwork

The certainty of our salvation!

Many religious faiths are built on the idea that you must earn your way to heaven. They teach that you can't be certain of where you will go when you die. Therefore, you need to do more and more things for God. Hopefully, you will please God and he will let you in. **Read 1 John 5:11-13.** Why did John write this? How should knowing that you have eternal life affect the way you live right now? What would you tell someone who told you that "it is arrogant to claim with certainty that you are going to heaven"?

Here are some more great verses on the same topic for you to reflect on!

Romans 8:1-2
1 Corinthians 1:8-9
Galatians 2:16
Ephesians 1:3-4 (or all of chapter 1!)
Philippians 1:3-6

Helping each other

How can we help each other when one of us doubts that God loves them?

How can we stay confident that we will go to heaven when we die?

let's pray

- Thank God for his love for us.
- Thank God for his promises towards us.
- Pray that we will keep trusting in Jesus.
- Pray for anyone you know who is experiencing doubt about God.
- *Other things we can pray for* ______________________________

____

stay tuned

Next week we will look at what we do if we want to follow Jesus but we still sin!

For your eyes only:
The week ahead

For your eyes only:
The Week ahead

1. Personal Bible Reading

If you are reading the gospel of Mark, try and read chapters 9-12 this week.

My weekly Bible reading plan!

In the gospel of Mark I read (place a ✔ when you have read it!)

Chapter 9 ☐ Chapter 10 ☐ Chapter 11 ☐ Chapter 12 ☐

FYI

Who wrote the Bible? Who was it written for? As you have read earlier, the Bible is a collection of 66 books. Each of these was written for a particular reason. There are a number of people who wrote a large number of the books (for example: Paul, Luke, and John). While other authors wrote just one (example: Isaiah, James and Jude). There are a number of different reasons why the various books of the Bible were written. Some were written to give a record of the life of Jesus, others to answer questions; some to warn believers to be careful of false teachers, others to encourage believers in the Christian faith. Quite often the books will tell you why they are written and who they were written for.

Read the Bible passages below and try to figure out who wrote each book, and why they were written.

Luke 1:1-4 ______________________________

John 20:30-31 ______________________________

Galatians 1:1-9 ______________________________

Jude v. 3-4 ______________________________

Revelation 1:1-3 ______________________________

2. Memory Verse

Can you learn the memory verse at the start of the study (Rom. 10:9)? Give it a try this week.

If you declare with your mouth, "Jesus is Lord," and believe in your heart that God raised him from the dead, you will be saved.

Romans 10:9

3. Prayer

Pray that you will continue to follow Jesus.
Pray that this will give you hope each day.
Ask God to fill you with the certainty of salvation that Jesus gives us.
Pray that you will have the strength to share this with your friends.

Things that I can thank God for: ____________________

____

____

Things that I need to ask God to help me with: ____________________

____

____

Final words: Beware of the accuser!

The Bible warns us that we have an enemy. This enemy hates the fact that we can know we are going to heaven. Because of this, he is totally committed to our destruction. One of his secret weapons is to lie to us about whether or not God loves us. He also wants to make us feel guilty about the bad things we do. This enemy hates the study you have just done and wants to rob you of the certainty that you are going to heaven. Read these Bible verses below to arm yourself so that you can stand against this enemy!

John 10:7-10   Ephesians 6:10-18   1 Peter 5:8-11   Revelation 12:10-12

If we confess our sins, he is faithful and just and will forgive us our sins and purify us from all unrighteousness. 1 John 1:9

let's get started

How do you feel when you do something that you know is wrong?

- I ignore my feelings
- I just wait for the bad feeling to go away
- I have a good cry
- I never do anything wrong!
- I take it out on my little brother/sister
- I tell God how I feel
- I say "I'm sorry" and hope for the best
- I don't care
- Something else ______________

Have you ever been caught doing something wrong? What happened?

going deeper

The Bible says that everyone does things they shouldn't (this is called "sin"). Read 1 John 1:8-9.

What does this say about someone who says, "Me? I'm not a sinner"? (v. 8)

What does this tell us we must do when we do something that is wrong? (v. 9)

What happens when we ask God for forgiveness?

Hold on just a minute! Does this mean that I can sin whenever I want to? Here are two common responses people make when they find out God will forgive us when we sin:

"Hey, it's ok to sin- God will forgive me!"

"God doesn't care about what I do."

How would you respond to these statements?

We can't "just sin whenever we want to"! Read Romans 6:15-18.
How is sinning similar to being a "slave"?

What do you think it means to be a "slave to righteousness"?

So, what does this passage teach a Christian who says, "Sin doesn't matter, God will forgive me?"

brainwork **Jesus is our "heavenly lawyer"!**
Have you ever been in a situation where you needed someone to come and help you? What happened? The Bible says that Jesus is our help when we sin. He is, in a way, our "heavenly lawyer"!
Read 1 John 2:1-2.

What does God do so that we can have forgiveness for our sins?

What does this mean for us when we don't do what is right?

Think about when you've done things that you know were wrong. What should your response now be?

Helping each other

How can we help each other to avoid sin? Write down 2 or 3 helpful tips and then share them with the group.

1.

2.

3.

If there is still time, read Galatians 6:1-2 and answer these two questions:

How should we treat a friend who sins?

What must we be careful of?

Is there anything we must do differently in light of our study today?

let's pray

- Pray for strength to fight sin.
- Pray that we will be people who ask for God's forgiveness when we sin.
- *Other things we can pray for* ________________________________

____

(You may wish to spend a moment in silent prayer and ask for forgiveness for anything that you have done wrong in the last week or two.)

stay tuned

Next week we will look at what the Bible says about going the distance as a Christian. Is it possible to stay a Christian forever?

For your eyes only:
The week ahead

For your eyes only:
The Week ahead

1. Personal Bible Reading

It is important that you learn to ask for God's forgiveness each time you sin. Read Psalms 32 & 51 this week. These Psalms are "cries from the heart" of a man who had sinned before God and needed forgiveness. If you are reading the gospel of Mark, read chapters 13-16 this week.

My weekly Bible reading plan!

In the gospel of Mark I read (place a ✔ when you have read it!)

Chapter 13 ☐ Chapter 14 ☐ Chapter 15 ☐ Chapter 16 ☐

FYI

Reading the Bible

Some people mistakenly see the Bible as some sort of magic book. They will just open it up at any page and hope that there is a special message to them from God. The Bible was not written to be read like this, but was written to help and encourage believers in certain situations. It is important for you to not just pick and choose a verse or two but rather try and understand a whole section or book at a time. You may not be able to do this in one sitting, but over a week (or two) try and read a whole book of the Bible. The gospels are a good place to start. You may also want to try and read a bit of the Old Testament and a bit of the New Testament each day.

2. Memory Verse

Can you learn the memory verse at the start of the study (1 John 1:9)? Give it a try this week.

Pray this week that God would help you this week to avoid sin. However, realize that all Christians sin. The goal is to fight against sin and to seek God's forgiveness when it happens.

Things that I can thank God for: ______________________

____

____

Things that I need to ask God to help me with: ______________________

____

____

Are there some sins that you are particularly struggling with and need help for? If so, is there anyone you can talk to about it? Maybe this could be your youth leader, minister or an older Christian that you trust. See if you can make a time this week to chat with them about it. They may be able to give you some advice on how to fight this sin, pray with you, or help keep you accountable in this matter.

"Don't sit next to the fire if your head is made of butter!" Hot tips for fighting sin.

These famous words were said by Martin Luther (he was a famous church leader a long time ago). What he is saying is: don't stay close to things that will cause you to sin- especially if you struggle with them. Examples of these could be trashy magazines, friends who gossip, the Internet, or violent computer games.

Here are some things to help you sin less:

- Learn to identify your weaknesses. Get to know what causes you to sin and then try your best to stay away from those things.
- Have an "accountability partner". This is someone you can be honest with and who can help you to avoid mistakes. They must be someone you can trust and who will not talk to others about what you share with them.
- Pray for God to give you strength to avoid sin.
- If you have friends who aren't Christians and want you to sin with them, it may be time to look around for some new friends!

Starting Out: Don't give up! How to persevere as a Christian

We must pay more careful attention, therefore, to what we have heard, so that we do not drift away. Hebrews 2:

(FYI The word "persevere" means to stay with something. It is the opposite of quitting!)

let's get started

What is one (or more!) thing you have started but not finished?

- ☐ music lessons
- ☐ getting in shape
- ☐ cleaning my room
- ☐ reading a book
- ☐ fixing something
- ☐ building/making something
- ☐ something else ____________________

Why didn't you finish it? Is there something else that you've stayed with for a long time? What is it?

____

____

Warning! Warning! It is very serious to turn away from Jesus!

Read: Hebrews 3:12-14.

What do you think it means to have a "sinful, unbelieving heart"? (v.12)

What are we to do to keep this from happening? (v.13)

What does v.14 tell us we must aim for?

Be careful of "spiritual heart disease"!

The image in Hebrews 3:12-14 is like a person whose heart is slowly turning to stone. As it hardens, it turns away from the living God. The pattern for most people who stop following Jesus is not to do it suddenly, but to slowly drift away (see Hebrews 2:1).

Have you ever known anyone who has stopped being a Christian? Why did they stop?

Your personal "checklist"

Place a ✔ next to anything you think could cause you to slowly drift away from Jesus.

- ◯ sport
- ◯ the opposite sex
- ◯ school (& homework etc.)
- ◯ music
- ◯ non-Christian friends
- ◯ trying to be popular
- ◯ family
- ◯ being "too busy"
- ◯ getting a job / future career
- ◯ something else ____________________

What must you do to avoid letting these things pull you away?

Here are a number of helpful Bible verses that give us wisdom on how to persevere as a Christian. If there's not time to read them all now, try to finish reading them at home.

1 Corinthians 15:58 | Ephesians 5:15-20 | Philippians 2:12-13
Colossians 2:6-8 & 3:5-14 | Hebrews 10:25

brainwork **Spiritual arithmetic- keep adding these things and you won't go wrong! Read 2 Peter 1:1-11.**

What does God's power give us? (v.3)

There are seven things we are to add to our faith. (v.5-7). Write them down here:

1. ________________ 2. ________________ 3. ________________

4. ________________ 5. ________________ 6. ________________

7. ________________

Are there any words or ideas here that you don't understand?

What can we do each day to add these things to our life?

According to v.8, why are these things so important?

What do v.10 & 11 tell us will happen if we do these things?

getting active

Helping each other

How can this group help each other to follow Jesus forever? Spend a minute and come up with a few things we can do straight away. (After a minute or so share them with each other.)

How should we react to anything that can threaten our commitment to Jesus?

let's pray

- Pray that we will stay Christians no matter what happens.
- Pray that we will be tough on things that could cause us to drift away from Jesus.
- Pray for any of our friends who may be wandering away from Jesus.
- *Other things we can pray for*

____

____

stay tuned For another great Bible study next week!

For your eyes only:
The week ahead

For your eyes only:
The Week ahead

1. Personal Bible Reading

This week read the book of 2 Peter. This is a great book filled with advice about how to stay a Christian forever. (If you are reading the gospel of Mark and haven't yet finished, see if you can finish it this week.)

My weekly Bible reading plan!

In the book of 2 Peter I read (place a ✔ when you have read it!)

Chapter 1 ☐ Chapter 2 ☐ Chapter 3 ☐

2. Memory Verse

Can you learn the memory verse at the start of the study (Hebrews 2:1)? Give it a try this week.

We must pay more careful attention, therefore, to what we have heard, so that we do not drift away. Hebrews 2:1

3. Prayer

It is important to always pray for strength to resist those things that can cause us to drift away. Pray also that you will not get entangled in any sin that will keep you away from Jesus. Pray this for your friends as well.

Things that I can thank God for: ____________________

____

____

Things that I need to ask God to help me with: ____________________

____

____

Hot Tips for Staying a Christian:

You have seen that it is very important to keep on following Jesus. Here are some "tips" to help you.

1. Make sure you meet with Christians regularly. Youth group, weekly Bible study and church are sure ways to help keep you on track. Almost every single person who drifts away from Jesus stops meeting with other Christians along the way. Remember Hebrews 3:13; we need to keep encouraging each other to stay with the faith.
2. Be disciplined in your Bible reading. This will keep reminding you of the greatness of God and how important it is to stay on the right path.
3. Be careful of friends who pull you away from Jesus. Believe it or not, some people are keen to see you stop following Jesus and join them in sin. 1 Corinthians 15:33 says, "Do not be misled: Bad company corrupts good character." If you are hanging with "bad company", you may not follow Jesus for long!
4. Stay alert! Stay vigilant! Quite often, the person who is not concerned with drifting away is the very person who drifts! The fact that you are on your guard is a very good thing. (See 1 Peter 5:8-9.)
5. Keep praying that you will never drift away.
6. Heed the warnings! Here are some more Bible passages that are on the topic of staying a Christian for the long haul. It would be wise to spend some time studying these excellent passages. Make sure you ask for God's help as you do this. Luke 9:57-62 and 14:25-35; Hebrews 5:11-6:12 & chapters 10 & 12; 2 Peter 1: 1-1.

Consider it pure joy, my brothers, whenever you face trials of many kinds, because you know that the testing of your faith develops perseverance. James 1:2-

Has anyone ever harassed you for any reason? If so, what was the situation?

If someone gave me a hard time for being a Christian I would...

- ○ cry
- ○ walk away
- ○ challenge them to a fight
- ○ get my big brother
- ○ pray
- ○ try and humiliate them
- ○ be kind to them
- ○ run away and hide
- ○ buy a mask
- ○ something else ______________

If you are insulted for following Jesus you are blessed!
Read Matthew 5:11-12.
What are three things that Jesus says may happen to you?

1. ______________________________
2. ______________________________
3. ______________________________

What will happen to you on the Day of Judgment because of this?

In light of these words from Jesus what would you say to someone who was getting harassed for being a Christian?

Stand firm in the face of persecution! Read Hebrews 10:32-39.
What was happening to the Christians when this was written? (v.32-34)

What will happen to us if we stand firm and stay Christian? (v.35-36)

What is our motivation for staying Christian according to v.37?

What does the writer of this letter expect from Christians? (v.39.)

brainwork

Consider suffering as a joy!

Have you ever gone through a tough time and thought about not being a Christian anymore? What happened? **Read James 1:2-4.** Why are we to consider tough times to be a good thing? (Read v. 3 for help.)

___

What is the "finished work" of perseverance? (v. 4)

___

How can you start seeing suffering for Jesus as a joy instead of a burden?

___

___

getting active

getting active

Helping each other

How can we help each other to live out what these parts of the Bible say?

Is there anything we must do differently this week in light of our study today?

let's pray

- Pray that we will continue with Jesus even when times are tough.
- *Other things we can pray for*

___

___

___

For your eyes only:
The week ahead

For your eyes only:
The Week ahead

1. Personal Bible Reading

This week choose a book of the Bible and try to read the whole thing. If you need a suggestion, read James. This is a book full of wisdom about how to live as a Christian. (If you are reading the gospel of Mark and haven't finished, finish it this week.)

My weekly Bible reading plan!

In the book of James I read (place a ✔ when have you read it!)

Chapter 1 ☐ Chapter 2 ☐ Chapter 3 ☐ Chapter 4 ☐ Chapter 5 ☐

2. Memory Verse

Can you learn the memory verse at the start of the study (James 1:2-3)? Give it a try this week.

Consider it pure joy, my brothers, whenever you face trials of many kinds, because you know that the testing of your faith develops perseverance. James 1:2-3

Continue to pray for strength when following Jesus gets tough. Pray this for your friends as well.

Things that I can thank God for: ______________________

____

____

____

Things that I need to ask God to help me with: ______________________

____

____

____

thank you

Thanks to Belinda Hopper and Susie Ley for their proofreading editing.
Thanks also to Sarah van Delden for her work on the layout and graphics.

Other recommended resources for your youth ministry:

Small group Bible Studies

Foundations For Christian Living
By Ken Moser

Young Men
By Ken Moser

Young Women
By Julie Moser

Luke: Who Is Jesus?
By Ken Moser

Luke: Jesus' Parables
By Ken Moser

Luke: Carry Your Cross
By Ken Moser

Death And Resurrection Of Jesus
By Julie Moser

Work Rest Play
By Ken Moser

Big Issues For Today's Youth
By Ken Moser

Studies 2 Go
By Julie Moser

More Studies 2 Go
By Julie Moser

Resources for leaders

Programs 2 Go
By Ken Moser

Changing the World through Effective Youth Ministry
By Ken Moser

Creative Christian Ideas for Youth Groups
By Ken Moser

Youth Evangelism: Reaching Young People in a Way that Honours God
By Ken Moser